THE

GENTLEMAN'S

PUZZLE BOOK

THE GENTLEMAN'S PUZZLE BOOK

Summersdale Publishers Ltd
46 West Street
Chichester
West Sussex
PO19 1RP
UK

www.summersdale.com

Printed and bound in the Czech Republic

ISBN: 978-1-84953-594-6

Substantial discounts on bulk quantities of Summersdale books are available to corporations, professional associations and other organisations. For details contact Nicky Douglas by telephone: +44 (0) 1243 756902, fax: +44 (0) 1243 786300 or email: nicky@summersdale.com.

THE
GENTLEMAN'S
PUZZLE BOOK

NEIL SOMERVILLE

summersdale

Other Puzzle books by the author:

The Lady's Puzzle Book
The British Puzzle Book

Dedicated to Don Somerville,
a fine and redoubtable gentleman

INTRODUCTION

My first makes company,
My second shuns company,
My third assembles company,
My whole puzzles company.
What am I?

Welcome to *The Gentleman's Puzzle Book*. This little conundrum above is just one of the many types of puzzles you will find in the following pages to tickle your brain and put your problem-solving skills to the test. Whether you enjoy sudokus, criss crosses, anagrams, coded crosswords or considering the meaning of splendid words such as 'mirligoes' and 'bullimong', there is much here to amuse, entertain and perplex.

Before the fun begins, have you worked out the above conundrum? If not, the answer is just that: conundrum (co-nun-drum).

Good luck and happy puzzling, gentlemen.

Neil Somerville

MEN OF LETTERS

The following anagrams conceal the names of
distinguished writers from across the centuries.
Who are they?

1. Hoards a myth

2. Shan't joke

3. Me? As I sparkle a while

4. I am lean

5. Had dollar

HIDDEN NAMES

A male first name is hidden somewhere in each of the following sentences. What is it? In the following example, 'He bought a newspaper and avidly read the report', the hidden name is David (an**d avid**ly).

1. Yes, I'm on track to finish this puzzle!

2. When I get to the end of the lane, I'll be half way.

3. If it gets colder, ice will be a real hazard.

4. He faced a difficult meeting at his club or isolation if he did not attend.

5. After serving two weeks as an apprentice, am on new duties and a far better wage.

WEIRD AND WONDERFUL

Our language contains many weird and wonderful words.
Which is the correct definition of each of the following?

1. Flummery

a) Shaggy dog story
b) Omen
c) Jelly made from oats

2. Napery

a) Thick scarf
b) Table linen
c) Spectacular bird formation

3. Whid

a) Move quickly
b) Rumour
c) Pothole in road

4. Yare

a) Ready
b) Skipping rope
c) Harness

WORD SEARCH: FISH

Many a gentleman is fond of fishing. Find the following in this anglers' word search – as well as one that got away and is not in the list. What and where is the elusive fish?

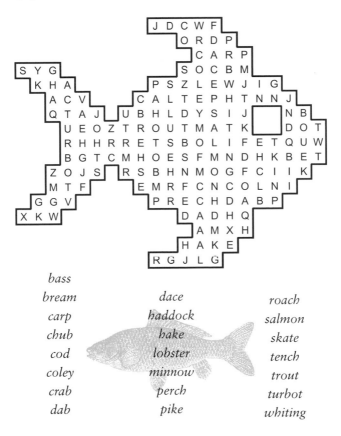

bass		
bream	dace	roach
carp	haddock	salmon
chub	hake	skate
cod	lobster	tench
coley	minnow	trout
crab	perch	turbot
dab	pike	whiting

CRYPTOGRAM

Solve the cryptogram to reveal the philosophical uttering
of a rather distinguished gentleman poet.
To help you start, W = C and B = M.

B	H	G	J	V	R		L	Z	B	J		T	E		R	H	I	P	T	R	F.
M									M												.

T'	G		V	Z	I	P	J	V		P	Z	M	J		Z	R		Z	W	V	J
'																			C		

H	L		K	Z	R	G.
						.

Z	K	L	V	J	G,		K	H	V	G		I	J	R	R	U	E	H	R
					,														

WORD LADDER

Many a gentleman appreciates a tipple, particularly a generous glass of good wine. Changing one letter at a time, turn the word 'good' into 'wine'.

Good

Wine

WORD QUEST

Make as many words as possible of four or more letters from the letters below. In making a word, each letter may be used only once and each word must always contain the central letter, C. A nine-letter word can also be made using all the letters and is something many a gentleman owns. No plurals allowed.

28 words excellent; 22 very good

MISSING WORDS

A four-letter word completes the first word or phrase and starts the second. So in 'sail _ _ _ _ team', the missing word would be 'away', making 'sail away' and 'away team'.

1. take _ _ _ _ book

2. draw _ _ _ _ miss

3. sure _ _ _ _ exit

4. slip _ _ _ _ room

5. blow _ _ _ _ time

MINI SUDOKU

How fast are you with sudoku – can you polish off this
one in timely fashion? Complete the grid so that every
row, column and 2x3 box contains the six letters that
make up the word 'timely'.

T				Y	
	Y	M			
		Y		M	
	T		L		
			I	T	
	M				E

CODED CROSSWORD

Each letter of the alphabet has been replaced by a number. To solve the puzzle, you must decide which letter is represented by which number. To help you start, one of the words has already been filled in.

13		15		14		1		9		11		10
16	2	20	24	9	26	10	3		11	17	19	2	25	3
	24		11		9		11		19		23		26
12	25	11	7	3	18	11	17	14	10		24	19	11	10
	6				8		14		3		19		19
14	3	25	19	11	26		10	3	9	3	6	26	13	10
			3		6		4				10		3
13	15	24	3	26	21	4		13	12	25	11	19	10	13
	24		20				16		3		2		
5	11	2	9	3	19	6	3		25	3	19	10	26	9
	22		3		11		25		18				16
8 B	2 O	13 S	13 S		19	3	6	25	2	12	2	9	11	13
	10		13		3		24		25		11		20
5	11	2	9	3	10		25	3	6	21	9	3	13	13
	6		4		4		4		3		13		10

1	2 O	3	4	5	6	7	8 B	9	10	11	12	13 S
14	15	16	17	18	19	20	21	22	23	24	25	26

TRACK WORD

Starting with the circled letter and moving one letter at a time, either horizontally or vertically, find seven things a gentleman may see or pass when taking a stroll down a city street.

(P)	O	F	E	N	S	A
T	S	A	C	E	W	G
B	O	O	P	T	N	E
B	X	T	C	S	T	T
U	S	S	H	L	I	E
L	L	O	O	Y	N	R
I	B	R	A	R	I	B

A PERPLEXING POSER

What do you throw
out when you want to
use it, but take in when you
don't want to use it?

SUDOKU

Complete all the squares so that each row, column and each of the 3x3 squares contains all the digits from one to nine.

6			4			1		
	5			1	6		2	
			7					3
7						9	5	
	1	6		4		3	7	
	4	3						2
4				8				
	8		7	6			4	
		1			4			7

CRYPTOGRAM

Solve the cryptogram to give an amusing thought.
To give you a start, B = U and K = L.

I	W	T		I	Y		Z	S	T		C	T	X	Z		Z	S	N	W	V	X

M		J	M	W		L	M	W		S	M	G	T		B	Q		S	N	X
															U					

X	K	T	T	G	T		N	X		M		Y	B	W	W	A	-	C	I	W	T.
	L												U				-				.

ANAGRAMS

All these anagrams are in some way connected with motoring and the hazards thereof. What are they?

1. Pre-marketing

2. Is flight craft

3. Decrease map

4. Or ask word?

5. Am too wry

ACROSTICS

Solve the clues correctly and the words in the shaded columns will spell out an esteemed quality of a gentleman.

1					
2					
3					
4					
5					
6					

1. *Rostrum*
2. *Canadian capital*
3. *Changed lenses brings decrease*
4. *Attack as false or wrong*
5. *Chewy sweet*
6. *One or the other*

MATCHSTICK PUZZLE

Make a square by moving just one matchstick.

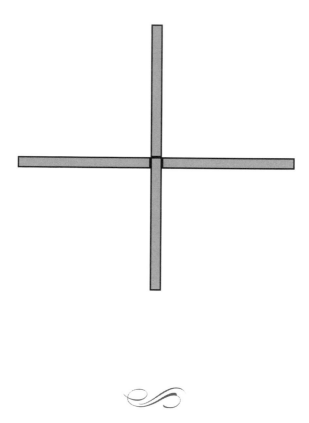

WORD QUEST

Make as many words as possible of four or more letters from the letters below. In making a word, each letter may be used only once and each word must always contain the central letter, K. A nine-letter word can also be made using all the letters.

41 words excellent; 34 words very good

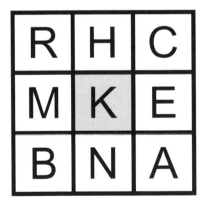

WEIRD AND WONDERFUL

Which is the correct definition of each of the following
weird and wonderful words?

1. Bedight

a) To startle
b) To decorate
c) Makeshift tent

2. Mirligoes

a) Carnival float
b) Ornate ribbon
c) Dizziness

3. Popple

a) To bob up and down
b) To create a fuss
c) Fastener

4. Hoker

a) To ridicule
b) Crumbling cliff
c) Coal bucket

MYSTERY SUDOKU

Complete the grid so that every row, column and 3x3 box contains the letters ACHLORSTU in any order. One row or column contains a seven-letter word which can be applied to an erudite gentleman. What is it?

	R			A			O	
L			H				U	C
C		O				L		
	U			L				
			R		T			
				C			S	
		A				O		R
S	H				R			T
	L			H			A	

WORD BUILDER

The letters of a nine-letter word have been numbered one to nine. Solve the clues to discover what it is: something that many a dashing gentleman likes to wear.

Letters 7, 2, 6 and 5 give an outer garment.

Letters 8, 6, 4, 5 and 9 lead us to hurry.

Letters 1, 3, 4 and 9 cause us to ponder and reflect.

Letters 7, 8, 3 and 1 give us a good friend.

Letters 8, 2 and 9 give us a gardening tool.

What is the word?

1	2	3	4	5	6	7	8	9

ANT-ICS

The answers to the following clues are words ending in 'ant'. The number of letters in the word is given in brackets after the clue. As an example, a hibernating ant (7) would be dormant.

1. A baby ant (6)

2. A pouring out ant (6)

3. A warlike ant (8)

4. An unknowing ant (8)

5. An unremitting ant (9)

6. A stale, still ant (8)

CROSSWORD

Across

6 Popular dessert (7)
7 Come into effect (5)
9 Threesome (4)
10 Plant grown for beauty (10)
11 National sport (8)
13 Landing strip (6)
15 Pain (4)
17 Punctuation (5)
18 Developed (4)
19 Gentleman's adornment (3,3)
20 Business suit (3-5)
23 Expert (10)
26 Mite mix this unit (4)
27 Pub game (5)
28 A pair (7)

Down

1 Mixture (10)
2 Asian temple (6)
3 Garden of paradise (4)
4 Popular liqueur (3,5)
5 Revolve (4)
6 Freight (5)
8 Proceed to mix this mean tea (7)
12 Best not exceed (5)
14 Trifling (10)
16 Cut into pieces (7)
17 Fissure (8)
21 Yield (6)
22 Peak (5)
24 Moderate (4)
25 Irritation (4)

WORD SEARCH: THE GENTLEMAN'S PUZZLE BOOK

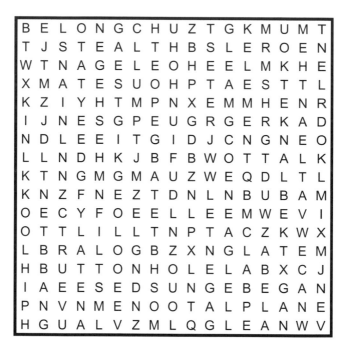

```
B E L O N G C H U Z T G K M U M T
T J S T E A L T H B S L E R O E N
W T N A G E L E O H E E L M K H E
X M A T E S U O H P T A E S T T L
K Z I Y H T M P N X E M M H E N R
I J N E S G P E U G R G E R K A D
N D L E E I T G I D J C N G N E O
L L N D H K J B F B W O T T A L K
K T N G M G M A U Z W E Q D L T L
K N Z F N E Z T D N L N B U B A M
O E C Y F O E E L L E E M W E V I
O T T L I L L T N P T A C Z K W X
L B R A L O G B Z X N G L A T E M
H B U T T O N H O L E L A B X C J
I A E E S E D S U N G E B E G A N
P N V N M E N O O T A L P L A N E
H G U A L V Z M L Q G L E A N W V
```

All the following words can be made out of the letters of the title, *The Gentleman's Puzzle Book* – but can this gentleman find them all in the puzzle? There is also one word hidden in the puzzle not included in the list. What is the mystery word, something a patriotic gent may enjoy singing?

agent	*glean*	*pen*
along	*house*	*plane*
bat	*laugh*	*platoon*
began	*lent*	*shell*
belong	*look*	*stealth*
bet	*lump*	*sun*
blanket	*meet*	*tell*
buttonhole	*metal*	*tent*
eagle	*mull*	*test*
elegant	*nest*	*zeal*
element	*oblong*	*Zen*
gleam	*peg*	*zest*

CODED CROSSWORD

Each letter of the alphabet has been replaced by a number. To solve the puzzle, you must decide which letter is represented by which number. To help you start, one word has been partly filled in.

24		26		3		4		7		23		11	
12	26	18	4	6	25		11	2	8	4	2	14	25	16
5		4		6		6		26		1		19	
9	11	19	3 C	23	21	26	10		19	2	19	25	14	16
16		6 U		25		7		14		26		8	
9	11	24	19 T	8	11		11	16	9	2	8	2	24	13
18				24		1				2			
11	1	19	8	2	16	14		19	14	11	3	11	17	14
		2				11		1				2	
4	8	14	24	20	2	14	16		7	8	2	9	25	18
11		13		24		15		26		9		26	
20	2	7	7	14	8		14	22	6	2	7	11	13	14
1		6		6		8		1		11		8	
15	2	26	25	2	1	19	1		11	2	8	5	11	18
24		25		23		14		25		19		9	

1	2	3 C	4	5	6 U	7	8	9	10	11	12	13
14	15	16	17	18	19 T	20	21	22	23	24	25	26

ANAGRAMS

Solve these anagrams to discover items you may see
displayed in a stately home.

1. Gains pint

2. To manners

3. Enriches lad

4. Damsel

5. Got posh harp

MINI SUDOKU

A bowler hat has long been an accoutrement of choice for the city gent. Complete the grid so that every row, column and 2x3 box contains the six letters that make up the word 'bowler'.

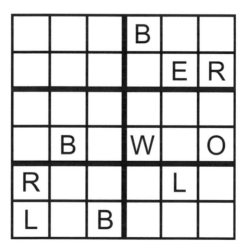

WORD LADDER

While enjoying a spot of recreation in the great outdoors, a resourceful gentleman may turn his hand to making a camp fire. Changing one letter at a time, turn the word 'camp' into 'fire'.

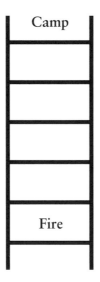

WORD SEARCH: EUROPEAN TOUR

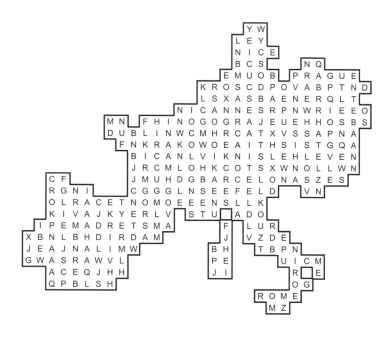

In the mood for a jaunt around Europe? Take a tour round the puzzle to find the following destinations. There is also a mystery location not included in the list. What and where is it?

Amsterdam

Madrid

Athens

Milan

Barcelona

Monaco

Basel

Monte Carlo

Berlin

Moscow

Bruges

Munich

Brussels

Naples

Budapest

Nice

Cannes

Paris

Cologne

Prague

Copenhagen

Reykjavik

Dublin

Rome

Florence

Salzburg

Geneva

Seefeld

Ghent

Seville

Helsinki

Stockholm

Krakow

Verona

Lisbon

MATCHSTICK PUZZLE

Move two matches to create six squares.

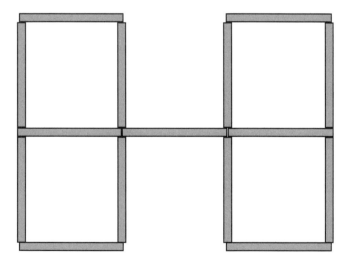

CRYPTOGRAM

Solve the cryptogram to discover the mystery sentences.
To give you a start, B = M and F = P.

M		K	Z	W	N	T	Z	B	M	W		H	W		M		N	O	M	V	W		V	G
								M																

G	N	E	U	C	V	W	K		N	I	V	G		J	H	H	L.		I	V	G
																	.				

F	E	Y	Y	T	Z	U		T	H	H	L		B	Z	T	N	G		V	W	N	H
P													M									

M		G	B	V	T	Z		M	W	U		I	Z		N	E	O	W	G
			M																

N	I	Z		F	M	K	Z.
				P			.

MYSTERY SUDOKU

Complete the grid so that every row, column and 3x3 box
contains the letters AFHIMNORU in any order. One row
or column contains a seven-letter word which is suitable
for an officer and a gentleman. What is it?

R	F		M	I				
						I	N	
	I				H		M	U
	M			A		R		
			U		M			
		I		O			H	
F	H		R				O	
	U	A						
				N	A		F	H

WEIRD AND WONDERFUL

Which is the correct definition of the following?

1. Fribble

a) A shiver
b) To tease
c) A trifling action

2. Celsitude

a) Eminence
b) Temper tantrum
c) Evasiveness

3. Harl

a) Walking stick
b) Fibre of flax
c) A draft

4. Smir

a) To deceive
b) Fine rain
c) Burnt cooking odour

HIDDEN NAMES

A gentleman's first name is hidden in each of the
sentences. Can you spot it?

1. You were really gallant on your first
   attempt and showed great style.

2. His new approach was beneficial and
   successful.

3. As a skilled diplomat he knew how to
   bypass the awkward question.

4. His first ever high jump broke the county
   record.

5. After a helping hand, am on target to
   achieve the results I desired.

TRACK WORD

Starting with the circled letter and moving one letter at
a time, either horizontally or vertically, track down eight
tools a gentleman is likely to keep in his toolbox
or garden shed.

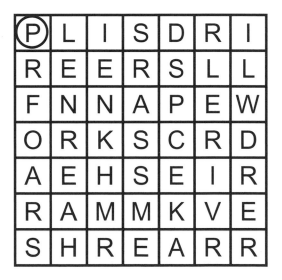

(P)	L	I	S	D	R	I
R	E	E	R	S	L	L
F	N	N	A	P	E	W
O	R	K	S	C	R	D
A	E	H	S	E	I	R
R	A	M	M	K	V	E
S	H	R	E	A	R	R

WORD SEARCH: FOOTBALL TEAMS

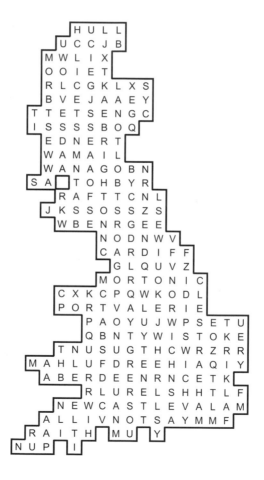

```
        H U L L
        U C C J B
      M W L I X
      O O I E T
      R L C G K L X S
      B V E J A A E Y
    T T E T S E N G C
    I S S S S B O Q
    E D N E R T
    W A M A I L
    W A N A G O B N
  S A   T O H B Y R
      R A F T T C N L
    J K S S O S S Z S
      W B E N R G E E
          N O D N W V
          C A R D I F F
          G L Q U V Z
        M O R T O N I C
    C X K C P Q W K O D L
    P O R T V A L E R I E
        P A O Y U J W P S E T U
        Q B N T Y W I S T O K E
      T N U S U G T H C W R Z R R
  M A H L U F D R E E H I A Q I Y
    A B E R D E E N R N C E T K
        R L U R E L S H H T L F
      N E W C A S T L E V A L A M
      A L L I V N O T S A Y M M F
    R A I T H   M U   Y
  N U P   I
```

Many a chap likes to indulge in a friendly game of footer, or show support for his home side. In this word search, find the following British teams – and which is the mystery team not included in the list?

Aberdeen

Arsenal

Aston villa

Bolton

Brighton

Burnley

Cardiff

Celtic

Dundee

Falkirk

Hearts

Hull

Ipswich

Leeds

Livingston

Morton

Newcastle

Norwich

Port Vale

QPR

Raith

Rangers

Stoke

Swansea

Tottenham

Watford

West Brom

West Ham

Wigan

Wolves

MISSING WORDS

A five-letter word completes the first word or phrase
and starts the second. What are the words?

1. direct _ _ _ _ _ march

2. heavy _ _ _ _ _ plate

3. wrong _ _ _ _ _ event

4. Tudor _ _ _ _ _ rules

5. valid _ _ _ _ _ taken

A PERPLEXING POSER

To complete the sentence describing an unfortunate incident, fill the blanks with the same letters in the same order:

The _____ surgeon was _____ to do the operation because he had _____.

CRISS CROSS: APPAREL

The following items of apparel might well be found in the wardrobe of a well-dressed gentleman. Fit the listed items into the grid.

3-letter word
hat

4-letter word
belt

5-letter words
beret
coats
boots
derby
jeans
scarf
shoes
socks

6-letter words
boater
bowler
braces
cravat
fleece
jersey
shirts
shorts
trilby
tweeds

7-letter word
sweater

8-letter words
bathrobe
flannels
trainers

10-letter words
cummerbund
eton jacket
lounge suit

12-letter word
business suit

ANAGRAMS

Unscramble the following anagrams to reveal some
well-known first names for gents.

1. Also chin

2. Lean crew

3. Met what?

4. Cherish port

5. Air atlas

MINI SUDOKU

At one time many a gentleman not only owned a bow tie but knew how to tie it. In this mini sudoku, complete the grid so that every row, column and 2x3 box contains the six letters that spell 'bow tie'.

	B				T
	I			O	
E			W		
	T			I	B

WORD LADDER

For those who follow the pugilist sports, a powerful left hook can be an awesome sight. In this word ladder, changing one letter at a time, turn left into hook.

Left

Hook

ANT-ICS

The answers to the following clues are words ending in 'ant'. The length of each word is given in brackets after the clue.

1. An irritable, tetchy ant (8)

2. A leftover ant (7)

3. A competitive ant (10)

4. An important, substantial ant (11)

5. A very costly ant (10)

6. A self-important, overbearing ant (8)

MYSTERY SUDOKU

Complete the grid so that every row, column and 3x3 box contains the letters ACEHILMRT in any order. One row or column contains a seven-letter word, something a gentleman who appreciates the arts might enjoy.
What is it?

		M	H					L
	I			R	L	A		
					E		C	
A		E		C		M		
		T		I		L		R
	A		M					
		R	A	H			M	
E					I	R		

WEIRD AND WONDERFUL

Which is the correct definition of each of the following weird and wonderful words?

1. Loosestrife

a) Omen

b) 'Couldn't care less' attitude

c) Plants of primrose family

2. Churl

a) Sour milk

b) Rustic labourer

c) Cowardly action

3. Pettifogger

a) Trickster

b) Moaner

c) Quibbling lawyer

4. Twinter

a) Two-year-old animal

b) Knowing wink

c) To speak quickly

CODED CROSSWORD

To solve the puzzle, you must decide which letter of the alphabet is represented by which number. To help you start, one of the words has been partly filled in.

	10	23	3	6	18	20		9	2	15	23	2	8
	11		11		16		4		11		16		19
24	15	15	1		23	3	25	15	23	22	24	3	12	16
	4		23		20		16		2		19		5
19	4	16	3	10	16		4	15	24	15	10	11	16	20
	18				24		18		21		19		16
20 (S)	19 (I)	14 (X)	1	18	13	15	23	8		18	15	15	26
			15				16				2		
	6	3	24	8		20	6	21	8	3	20	1	16	23
	23		16		7		2		16				14	
12	15	15	23	17	3	8	22		3	13	13	23	3	21
	2		3		24		24		11		19		4	
19	12	16	11	1	19	13	19	16	12		7	15	1	16
	16		4		20		4		16		16		24	
	23	16	16	24	16	12		1	23	2	20	1	21	

1	2	3	4	5	6	7	8	9	10	11	12	13
14 (X)	15	16	17	18	19 (I)	20 (S)	21	22	23	24	25	26

CRYPTOGRAM

Solve this cryptogram to reveal an astute observation
made by Henry Ward Beecher. To give you a start,
O = C, I = G and B = W.

O	R	Q	D	J	F	W		T	U	Z		H	T	U	U	F	A	W
C																		

Z	Q		U	Q	D		H	T	S	F		D	J	F		H	T	U;
																		;

Y	P	D		B	J	F	U		J	F		M	W		H	T	Z	F,
				W														,

D	J	F	N		I	A	F	T	D	R	N		M	H	X	A	Q	K	F
					G														

J	M	W		T	X	X	F	T	A	U	O	F.
											C	.

WORD SEARCH: ACTIVITIES AND PASTIMES

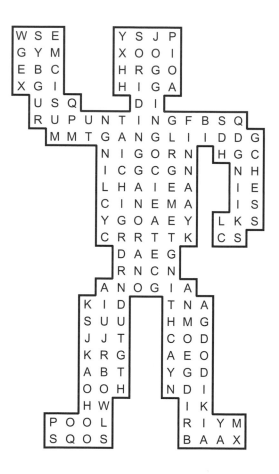

Active gents enjoy a wide variety of sports and hobbies, including the following eclectic list. Find them in the word search – together with one not included in the list. What is the mystery activity?

aikido	karate
art	music
bowls	pool
bridge	punting
chess	racing
cinema	riding
crib	rugby
cycling	singing
drama	T'ai chi
golf	tennis
gym	yachting
jogging	yoga
judo	

MATCHSTICK PUZZLE

Move four matchsticks to leave just two squares.

A PERPLEXING POSER

What occurs once in a minute, twice in a moment, but not once in a thousand years?

CROSSWORD

Across

6 Pear (7)
7 Selection (7)
9 Viper (5)
10 Ski hanger brings reduction (9)
11 Mix a height for this lofty repast (4,3)
13 Rejects (6)
15 Go through evenly (5,8)
18 Covering (6)
19 Action (7)
22 Transmit (9)
23 Nimble (5)
25 Ornamental badge of honour (7)
26 Disregard (7)

Down

1 Titled gent (4)
2 Vegetable (6)
3 Faithfulness (9)
4 Strong liquor (8)
5 Plan beforehand (10)
6 Indifference (6)
7 Another 1d (4)
8 Braided hair (5)
12 Colourful nursery (10)
14 Skilled (9)
16 Hasten (8)
17 Agree (6)
18 Hurling pole (5)
20 Colour (6)
21 Titled lady (4)
24 Notion (4)

WORD QUEST

Make as many words as possible of four or more letters from the letters in the box. In making a word, each letter may be used only once and each word must always contain the central letter, W. A nine-letter word can also be made using all the letters. No plurals allowed.

24 words excellent; 20 very good.

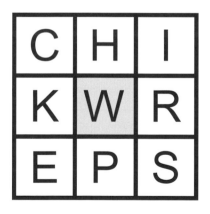

SUDOKU

Fill in all the squares so that each row, column and 3x3 square contains all the digits from one to nine.

		3	1					
					2	8		4
9		8			5			
					3	7		9
	1		5		4		3	
6		2	9					
			4			3		2
8		7	2					
					1	5		

MISSING WORDS

A five-letter word completes the first word or phrase
and starts the second.

1. razor _ _ _ _ _ frost

2. magic _ _ _ _ _ paper

3. steak _ _ _ _ _ party

4. grand _ _ _ _ _ score

5. small _ _ _ _ _ model

WORD BUILDER

The letters of a nine-letter word have been numbered one to nine. Solve the clues to discover a useful item some professional gents may own.

Letters 7, 8 and 1 give a curve

Letters 2, 6, 8 and 9 give a titled gentleman

Letters 8, 7, 4, 3 and 9 give something fast

Letters 1, 6, 5, 8 and 7 give a snake

Letters 5, 2, 3 and 4 give a radar signal

What is the word?

1	2	3	4	5	6	7	8	9

WORD SEARCH: COLLECTABLES

```
S S L I S S O F U K Z A P N S N T
B E I M D K I D U C C U S H N T R
F H L O S N E P N I A T N U O F I
E G L B E R E T G B H B K M I T N
J L P W M S Z A L G N C L O T E K
S S I E I I R X I L P O X D I A E
S N E L H B H E S S R M P E D S T
E K V H O S W T E C I P O L E P S
S E C X C R H H S I N A T C T O R
R O E O E T F P S M T C T A S O E
B S I P L C A N A A S T E R R N T
O C A D A C I W R R R S R S I S S
T P S B A O D I B E G E Y S F P O
T F T I C R I G Z C J O M W M V P
L N O I H S A F M I L I T A R I A
E X Y L T R A E N I F U T U C B N
S H S S R I N E V U O S F Y A P P
```

Do you have a nose for good collectables? Find the following items in the puzzle.

autographs

bottles

brasses

cameras

ceramics

cigar boxes

clocks

coins

compacts

dolls

fashion

fine art

fine wine

first editions

fossils

fountain pens

militaria

model cars

paperweights

posters

pottery

prints

radios

silver

souvenirs

stamps

teaspoons

thimbles

toys

trinkets

watches

ANAGRAMS

Solve these anagrams to discover the names of renowned musical and thespian gentlemen, past and present.

1. Award ledger (composer)

2. We avoid bid (pop star)

3. On any screen (actor)

4. Ideal caring (actor)

5. Capture my Clan (pop star)

TRACK WORD

Going one letter at a time, either horizontally or vertically, and starting with the circled letter, find seven different professions.

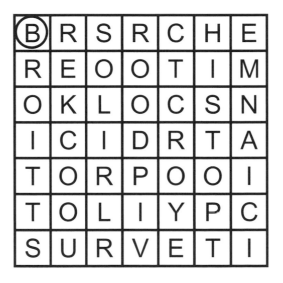

WORD LADDER

What better to refresh a chap than a tall glass of cold beer? Changing one letter at a time, transform 'cold' into 'beer'.

Cold
Beer

CRYPTOGRAM

Solve this cryptogram to discover an amusing remark by Mark Twain. To give you a start, X = F and Y = D.

D	E	A		X	N	H	A	M	D		J	G	Q	D	E	N	H	L
				F														

W	V	Y	A		N	M		V		Z	A	C	M	Q	H'	M		M	O	N	H,
		D																			,

S	R	D,		Q	X		J	Q	R	C	M	A,		M	Q	J	N	A	D	K
		,			F							,								

Y	A	W	V	H	Y	M		M	Q	W	A	D	E	N	H	L
D					D											

W	Q	C	A		D	E	V	H		D	E	N	M.
													.

WEIRD AND WONDERFUL

Which is the correct definition of each of the following
weird and wonderful words?

1. Fragor

a) Loud, sudden sound
b) Ditch
c) Disagreement

2. Helve

a) Ceremonial sword
b) Tool handle
c) Shepherd's shelter

3. Dizen

a) Draft
b) Candle extinguisher
c) Dress gaudily

4. Lentigo

a) Feeling faint
b) Spicy soup
c) Freckle

A PERPLEXING POSER

While out enjoying a stroll one summer day an observant gentleman crossed a bridge. As he did so he saw a boat full of people. Yet on the boat was not a single person. How could this be?

WORD QUEST

Make as many words as possible of four or more letters
from the letters below. In making a word, each letter may
be used only once and each word must always contain
the central letter, K. A nine-letter word can also be made
using all the letters.

26 words excellent; 21 words very good

MYSTERY SUDOKU

Complete the grid so that every row, column and 3x3 box contains the letters DENOPRTUX in any order. One row or column contains a seven-letter word denoting something which applies to many a gentleman. What is it?

					X		T	O
N			T		O		X	
		X		R		U		
E		T			U			P
			X		R			
U			D			N		X
		N		X		T		
	D		R		P			U
X	R		E					

MISSING LETTERS

The same three letters have been removed
from three words.

For example, in b _ _ _ k, f _ _ _ ch, and mil _ _ _ er, the
three letters removed were 'lin', with the words being
'blink', 'flinch' and 'milliner'.

Find the missing letters in the following:

1. L _ _ _ ing, d _ _ _ en, m _ _ _ ow.

2. Sc _ _ _ ture, presc _ _ _ t, st _ _ _ e

3. Br _ _ _ ly, qu _ _ _ r, he _ _ _ n

4. F _ _ _ er, al _ _ _ ed, g _ _ _ ingly

5. R _ _ _ ster, r _ _ _ on, strat_ _ _c

WORD LADDER

It can be a social occasion or an hour to savour alone,
but many a gentleman appreciates his meal time.
Changing one letter at a time, convert meal into time.

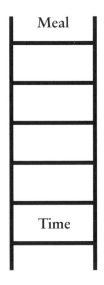

Meal

Time

ANAGRAMS

The following are anagrams of items a man of the world may wear, use or be required to have.

1. Bloke's cash

2. Decant jerkin

3. Sniff luck

4. Have RAF set

5. Pop stars

CODED CROSSWORD

Each letter of the alphabet has been replaced by a
number. To solve the puzzle, you must determine which
letter is represented by which number. To help you start,
one of the words has been filled in.

CRISS CROSS:
THE GENTLEMAN'S PUZZLE BOOK

All the following words can be made out of this book's title, *The Gentleman's Puzzle Book*. In this puzzle, fit them all in the grid.

3-letter words
bat
bet
let
peg
pen
sun
Zen

4-letter words
glen
hall
lent
look
lump
teal
tell
tent
test
zeal

5-letter words
began
eagle
gable
gleam
house
laugh
metal
phone

6-letter words
anthem
belong
lament
length
nettle
oblong

7-letter words
blanket
elegant
element
platoon
umpteen

10-letter word
puzzlement

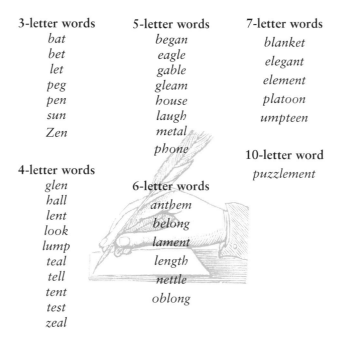

MATCHSTICK PUZZLE

By moving three matchsticks make three squares.

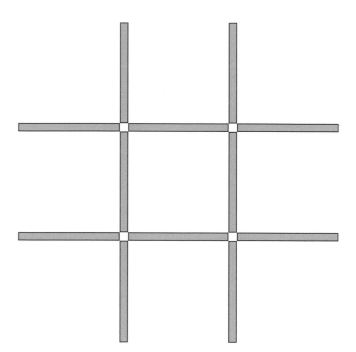

A PERPLEXING POSER

My first is in apple and also in pear,
My second is in desperate and also in dare,
My third is in sparrow and also in lark,
My fourth is in cashier and also in clerk,
My fifth is in seven and also in ten,
My whole is a blessing indeed unto men.

WEIRD AND WONDERFUL

What is the correct definition of each of the following weird and wonderful words?

1. Windlestraw

a) Large brimmed hat
b) Lanky person
c) Animal fodder

2. Kebbie

a) Unfounded rumour
b) Oatmeal cake
c) Shepherd's crook

3. Scrip

a) Small bag
b) Shortcut
c) Secret pact

4. Condiddle

a) Raucous dance
b) Nonsense poem
c) To steal

CRYPTOGRAM

Solve the cryptogram to discover a curious observation.
To give you a start, K = B and E = G.

D	S	X		Z	N	J		A	L	W	W		N		W	S	A		N	K	S	X	A
																			B			

N		O	L	W	W	S	H'	Y		Z	M	N	C	N	Z	A	L	C		K	D		M	V	Y
							'													B					

H	N	D		S	O		L	N	A	V	J	E		U	L	W	W	D	K	L	N	J	Y.
												G							B				.

C	S	J	N	W	Q		C	L	N	E	N	J
										G		

SUDOKU

Fill in all the squares so that each row, column and each
of the 3x3 squares contains all the digits from
one to nine.

					1			5
	3	9	2	7	4			
				8				7
8		6			3		5	
	1		6			3		8
4				1				
			7	6	2	5	1	
1			8					

WORD SEARCH

Hidden in this word search are 14 items you might find on a menu. What and where are they?

WORD LADDER

Many a gentleman welcomes the opportunity to slow down and enjoy a relaxing pursuit, perhaps doing one of these puzzles. In this word ladder, by changing one letter at a time, turn slow into down.

Slow

Down

WORD BUILDER

The letters of a nine-letter word have been numbered one to nine. Solve the clues to discover a quality a great many gentlemen would like to possess.

Letters 8, 4, 3 and 2 give us a brave and distinguished man

Letters 5, 8, 6, 3 and 9 give us a garment

Letters 7, 6, 1, and 9 give us a present.

Letters 7, 3, 6, 4 and 1 give us sorrow.

Letters 1, 2 and 7 give us a thick mist.

What is the word?

1	2	3	4	5	6	7	8	9

MINI SUDOKU

A trophy is a coveted possession of the successful gentleman. In this mini sudoku, complete the grid so that every row, column and 2x3 box contains the six letters that make up the word 'trophy'.

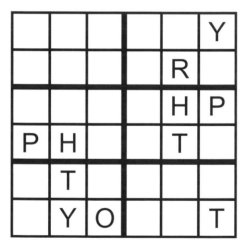

MEN OF LETTERS

The following are anagrams of some distinguished
writers, but who are they?

1. No anecdotal hurry

2. Check islanders

3. Almost handy

4. Naming life

5. So title

CODED CROSSWORD

Each letter of the alphabet has been replaced by a number. To solve the puzzle, you must decide which letter is represented by which number. To help you start, part of a word or phrase has been filled in.

	3 F		19		14		7		2		4		4	
1	19 O	13	3	15	17		26	9	15	26	17	15	8	5
	20 R		3		6		20		17		19		23	
25	26	16	14	7	12	26	8		17	6	9	15	6	23
	24		15		26		4		23		15		8	
18	19	20	16	4	21	4	24		19	8	4	23	5	4
	8						24		22		8			
26	5	20	19	15	8	23		14	4	20	16	26	6	8
			24		4		2						14	
10	7	13	24	6	14		20	4	12	4	12	2	4	20
	15		6		11		4		4		19		14	
10	20	4	3	26	2		26	17	17	4	5	19	20	13
	20		6		26		23		19		15		4	
7	26	22	4	17	8	15	16		23	19	17	17	26	20
	13		23		23		7		13		24		12	

1	2	3 F	4	5	6	7	8	9	10	11	12	13
14	15	16	17	18	19 O	20 R	21	22	23	24	25	26

TAKE AWAY

The names of two gentlemen have been mixed up in each of these clues. Take one away to find the other.

1. Take away one seafaring gentleman to leave another: **Hforranactiiosndrealsoken**

2. Take away one sportsman to leave another: **Sdteavivedrebdegcrkahvaem**

3. Take away one television character to leave another: **Bablsacilkfaawddlteyr**

4. Take away one writer to leave another: **Gecohrargelesodricwkeelnls**

5. Take away one actor to leave another: **Hcoulghingrfanirtht**

MYSTERY SUDOKU

Complete the grid so that every row, column and 3x3
box contains the letters AEGIKLNTV in any order. One
row or column contains a seven-letter word, a desirable
quality in certain items. What is it?

G			E		T	A		
A				L			V	N
	T		V		K			
E							G	A
		G		V				
V	I							K
		E		A		K		
I	A		L					V
		L	V		K			E

A PERPLEXING POSER

A gentleman is looking at a picture on the wall of his sitting-room. He says to a friend, 'I haven't any brothers or sisters, but that man's father was my father's son. Who is that man in the picture?

ACROSTICS

Solve the clues and with the two words in the shaded columns spell out something many a gentleman appreciates.

1						
2						
3						
4						
5						
6						

1. *Without depth*
2. *To be fond of*
3. *Paper folding*
4. *Long-winded*
5. *Models platform*
6. *Vacation*

CRYPTOGRAM

Solve the cryptogram to discover an amusing thought.
To give you a start, C = P and V = Y.

D	B	R	B	I	S		M	I		F	K	X	**O**	T		**B**	N

F	W	C	F	I	N	B	R	E,		A	G	O		B	O		Q	M	F	N
		P						,												

B	I	E	D	G	Q	F		K		P	X	F	F		O	X	B	C

K	X	M	G	I	Q		O	T	F		N	G	I		F	R	F	X	V		V	F	K	X.
																			Y		Y			.

WORD SEARCH: PARTY TIME

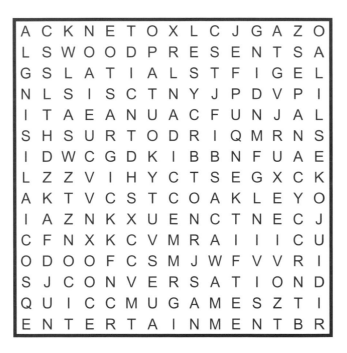

```
A C K N E T O X L C J G A Z O
L S W O O D P R E S E N T S A
G S L A T I A L S T F I G E L
N L S I S C T N Y J P D V P I
I T A E A N U A C F U N J A L
S H S U R T O D R I Q M R N S
I D W C G D K I B B N F U A E
L Z Z V I H Y C T S E G X C K
A K T V C S T C O A K L E Y O
I A Z N K X U E N C T N E C J
C F N X K C V M R A I I I C U
O D O O F C S M J W F V V R I
S J C O N V E R S A T I O N D
Q U I C C M U G A M E S Z T I
E N T E R T A I N M E N T B R
```

A jolly good time will be had by all if the following can be brought to the party. Can you find them in the puzzle? There is also a mystery word that has been omitted from the invitation list. What is it?

canapés
celebration
cocktails
conversation
dancing
drinks
entertainment
fancy dress
fun
games

gifts
invitations
jokes
laughter
music
presents
socialising
toasts
wine

WEIRD AND WONDERFUL

Which is the correct definition of each of these weird
and wonderful words?

1. Reave

a) Safety knot
b) Guttering
c) To rob

2. Broggle

a) To shove
b) To fish
c) Scarf

3. Pilgarlic

a) Bad tempered
b) Strong tasting
c) Bald person

4. Bullimong

a) Cattle feed
b) Walking stick
c) A sling or support

CODED CROSSWORD

Each letter of the alphabet has been replaced by a number. To solve the puzzle, you must determine which letter is represented by which number. To help you start, one of the words has been partly filled in.

1	2 T	3	4	5	6	7	8	9	10	11 U	12	13
14	15	16	17	18	19	20	21	22 O	23	24	25	26

MINI SUDOKU

Medals are a proud sign of military or sporting achievement for the distinguished gentleman. In this mini sudoku, complete the grid so that every row, column and 2x3 box contains the six letters that make up the word 'medals'.

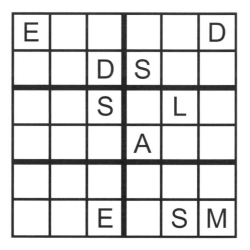

HIDDEN NAMES

A male first name is hidden in each of the sentences. What is the name?

1. Please put it on the tab as I'll pay for it all later.

2. The visitors admired the museum art. In particular, the bas reliefs much impressed.

3. After the masked wrestler's bear hug, he got a submission straightway and won the fight.

4. Let's hurry and we should be in time for the gala.

5. Looking at the calendar, Thursday was most convenient for the car service.

CRISS CROSS: GOLF

Time to tee off and, forgive the pun, 'putt' all these golfing words into the grid.

3-letter words
aim
par
tee

rough
slice
swing
wedge

4-letter words
chip
hole
hook
iron
putt
shot
wood

6-letter words
birdie
course
dogleg
driver
hazard
stroke

7-letter word
fairway

5-letter words
blade
bogey
buggy
eagle
green
links
pitch
range

8-letter words
golf ball
handicap

9-letter word
clubhouse

CRYPTOGRAM

Solve the cryptogram to reveal true words worth remembering. To give you a start, Z = M and P = B.

N	E	W		N	I		X	U	W		P	S	H	H	W	F	X
											B						

X	U	J	S	Q	Q	F		S	E		Q	S	I	W		M	N	Z	W	F
																		M		

I	J	N	Z		T	N	S	E	H		G		B	N	P		K	W	Q	Q.
			M												B					.

MISSING LETTERS

The same three letters have been removed from three words. What are the missing letters and words?

1. S _ _ _ rior, rec _ _ _ rate, gro _ _ _ d

2. V _ _ _ her, t _ _ _ an, t _ _ _ h

3. Dis_ _ _ se, des _ _ _ ate, re _ _ _ tory

4. Di _ _ _ ct, reve _ _ _ d, t _ _ _ nt

5. Cl _ _ _ c, inf _ _ _ ty, f _ _ _ sh

WORD SEARCH: YOUR GOOD HEALTH!

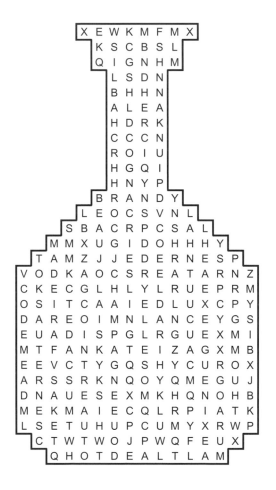

```
X E W K M F M X
K S C B S L
Q I G N H M
  L S D N
  B H H N
  A L E A
  H D R K
  C C C N
  R O I U
  H G Q I
  H N Y P
  B R A N D Y
  L E O C S V N L
  S B A C R P C S A L
  M M X U G I D O H H H Y
  T A M Z J J E D E R N E S P
V O D K A O C S R E A T A R N Z
C K E C G L H L Y L R U E P R M
O S I T C A A I E D L U X C P Y
D A R E O I M N L A N C E Y G S
E U A D I S P G L R G U E X M I
M T F A N K A T E I Z A G X M B
E E V C T Y G Q S H Y C U R O X
A R S S R K N Q O Y Q M E G U J
D N A U E S E X M K H Q N O H B
M E K M A I E C Q L R P I A T K
L S E T U H U P C U M Y X R W P
  C T W T W O J P W Q F E U X
  Q H O T D E A L T L A M
```

The drinks cabinet is brimming with tempting beverages. How many can you find in the bottle above? And what is the mystery tipple not included in the list?

Ale	Mead
Beaujolais	Medoc
Bordeaux	Moselle
Brandy	Muscadet
Burgundy	Port
Chablis	Riesling
Champagne	Rum
Cider	Sake
Cognac	Sauternes
Cointreau	Schnapps
Gin	Shandy
Hock	Sherry
Lager	Vodka
Madeira	

SUDOKU

Fill in all the squares so that each row, column and each
of the 3x3 squares contains all the digits from
one to nine.

7			1		5		9	
	9						5	
4					6			
8		6		7		2		
	3						7	
		2		4		6		9
			2					5
	1						4	
	4		9		3			1

A PERPLEXING POSER

This is a puzzle from long ago which has no doubt perplexed many a gentleman. What does the following message mean?

Y y u r y y u b i c u r y y for me.

MINI SUDOKU

Whether for a luxury long weekend or an active adventure, many a gentleman likes to travel. In this mini Sudoku, complete the grid so that every row, column and 2x3 box contains the six letters that make up the word 'travel'.

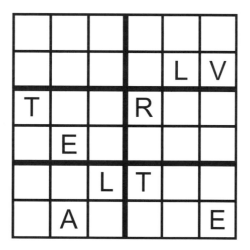

MYSTERY CROSSWORD

Solve the clues to discover something that can be a distinguishing feature of certain gents.

1	2	3	4	5
6				
7				
8				
9				

Across

1 *The distinguishing mystery feature*

6 *Express*

7 *French wine producing region*

8 *Transmits*

9 *Braid of hair*

Down

1 *Suddenly break apart*

2 *Colourless, volatile liquid*

3 *A note rearranged reconciles*

4 *Tears apart*

5 *Apparel*

CODED CROSSWORD

Each letter of the alphabet has been replaced by a number. To solve the puzzle, decide which letter is represented by which number. To help you start, one of the words has been filled in.

	25		26		23			6		6		8	
20	10	14	16	18	11	14	20		23	6	24	14	9	19
	9		18		9		7		11		3		19
12 J	5 U	3 G	23 S		25	19	6	8	6	19	6	24	20	6
	3				20		20		6		24		6
3	22	6	11	11	9		22	5	16	14	15	14	8	13
			2		20		19			6		6	
	4	5	14	20	21	11	6	16	25	6	19	6	15	
	5		24			25		9		6			
11	14	16	1	5	21	11	5		10	9	15	3	6	15
	17		6		18		1		18			24	
2	6	6	15	21	14	10	10	6	19		20	18	23	11
	19		15		23		14		14		18		5
15	6	10	6	11	6		20	18	11	6	3	9	19	13
	15		15		19			13		6		6	

1	2	3 G	4	5 U	6	7	8	9	10	11	12 J	13
14	15	16	17	18	19	20	21	22	23 S	24	25	26

A PERPLEXING POSER

Take away my first letter and
I remain unchanged.

Take away my second letter and
I remain unchanged.

Take away my third letter and
I remain unchanged.

Take away all my letters and
I will still be the same.

How can this be?

WORD LADDER

When shopping for the more unusual, many a gentleman hopes for a rare find. Changing one letter at a time, turn rare into find.

| Rare |
| |
| |
| |
| Find |
| |

HIDDEN NAMES

A male first name is hidden in each of the sentences. What is the name?

1. He would rather us sell the produce, than someone he did not know.

2. In the office there's a general phone for non-urgent calls.

3. The boy had to pay for the smashed window out of his pocket money.

4. Luckily the valuables lie hidden from view and only a few worthless items were taken.

5. After the first night, the show altered the format and became an overnight sensation.

WEIRD AND WONDERFUL

Which is the correct definition of the following weird
and wonderful words?

1. Noop

a) Darning needle
b) To pry
c) Sharp point of elbow

2. Yex

a) To puzzle over
b) Hiccups
c) Noisy disturbance

3. Forel

a) Book cover
b) Sheep pen
c) To guess

4. Keech

a) Lump of fat
b) Draft
c) Secret pact

WORD QUEST

Make as many words of four or more letters from the
letters below. In making a word, each letter may be used
only once and each word must always contain the central
letter, G. A nine-letter word can also be made using
all the letters.

33 words excellent; 27 words very good.

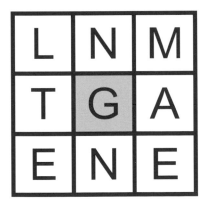

MISSING LETTERS

The same three letters have been removed from three words. What are the missing letters and words?

1. B _ _ _ on, d _ _ _ on, p _ _ _ e

2. B_ _ _ hely, humi _ _ _ y, mi _ _ _ ary

3. By _ _ _ d, re _ _ _ king, S _ _ _ d

4. Ba _ _ _ ng, soo _ _ _ ng, go _ _ _ c

5. S _ _ _ y, t _ _ _ id, w _ _ _ ied

ACROSTICS

Solve these clues and in the shaded squares will be a time of year quite a few sporting gentlemen look forward to.

1				
2				
3				
4				
5				
6				

1. Worth hazarding here?
2. Planned itinerary
3. Musical drama
4. Measures of alcohol perhaps?
5. Rearrange Oval's sudden outburst
6. Consumed

MYSTERY SUDOKU

Complete the grid so that every row, column and 3x3 box
contains the letters EGHLMORTU in any order. One row
or column contains a seven-letter word, applicable to a
discerning gentleman. What is it?

					O			M
		L	U	E	H			
	E		M	R		H		
	T		H			M	E	
	O						L	
	M	E			L		O	
		M		H	R		G	
			T	L	G	U		
E			O					

JUMBLED MOTORS

The names of various parts of the car have been merged
together. Remove one to find the other.

1. Adcacshelberaotaordr

2. Siegantitbioelnt

3. Sbtraekeredingrwuhemel

4. Craluditactohr

5. Hebaadtlitgerhyt

WORD SEARCH: ETIQUETTE

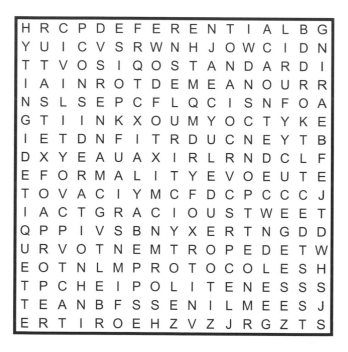

```
H R C P D E F E R E N T I A L B G
Y U I C V S R W N H J O W C I D N
T T V O S I Q O S T A N D A R D I
I A I N R O T D E M E A N O U R R
N S L S E P C F L Q C I S N F O A
G T I I N K X O U M Y O C T Y K E
I E T D N F I T R D U C N E Y T B
D X Y E A U A X I R L R N D C L F
E F O R M A L I T Y E V O E U T E
T O V A C I Y M C F D C P C C C J
I A C T G R A C I O U S T W E E T
Q P P I V S B N Y X E R T N G D D
U R V O T N E M T R O P E D E T W
E O T N L M P R O T O C O L E S H
T P C H E I P O L I T E N E S S S
T E A N B F S S E N I L M E E S J
E R T I R O E H Z V Z J R G Z T S
```

To decide the right thing to do in any situation, a gentleman may need recourse to the following. Can you find them in the puzzle?

bearing

civility

conduct

consideration

correctness

decency

decorum

deferential

demeanour

deportment

dignity

etiquette

formality

gracious

manners

poise

polish

politeness

proper

protocol

refinement

respect

rules

seemliness

standard

style

tact

taste

tone

CRYPTOGRAM

Solve this cryptogram to discover an amusing remark. To give you a start, K = J and O = B.

L		A	I	M	D	B	I		C	V		K	V	L	T		X	T	P		W	F	D	O
												J												B

C	U	X	C		G	V	D	F	Z		U	X	N	I		E	I		X	B

X		E	I	E	O	I	A.
					B		.

R	A	V	D	W	U	V		E	X	A	J

MISSING WORDS

The same word completes the first word or phrase and starts the second. The number of letters in the missing word is given in brackets.

1. Grand _ _ _ _ _ _ plan (6)

2. Local _ _ _ _ _ _ house (6)

3. Full _ _ _ _ _ _ _ time (7)

4. Stand _ _ _ _ _ life (5)

5. Court _ _ _ _ _ sense (5)

CRISS CROSS

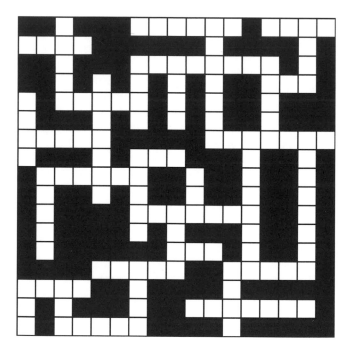

Fit the following names into the grid.

3-letter words

Ben

Bob

Don

Guy

Ian

Tom

Gavin

Geoff

Gerry

Keith

Nigel

Peter

Ralph

4-letter words

Andy

Fred

John

Leon

Mark

Neil

Paul

Rory

Toby

Walt

5-letter words

Barry

Derek

6-letter words

George

Jeremy

7-letter words

Frankie

Matthew

Maurice

Richard

William

8-letter words

Alastair

Jonathan

Laurence

CODED CROSSWORD

Each letter of the alphabet has been replaced by a number. To solve the puzzle, decide which letter is represented by which number. To help you start, one of the words has been filled in.

	14		11		5		11		3		9		24	
6 F	4 L	12 U	16 X		12	19	1	11	18	2	22	23	11	1
	17		22		24		3		11		19		19	
2	5	15	24	26	11		11	20	11	19	24	22	1	11
	25		21		2				19		11			
17	3	19	8	2	24	22	5		24	22	18	22	19	3
	12		4				4		11				11	
21	17	22	4		4	4	17	10	17		3	18	11	9
	18				8		22				11		18	
17	1	7	8	22	19		10	17	18	22	19	17	1	11
			21		11				12		11		8	
11	19	24	17	22	4	11	1		2	26	18	11	9	1
	22		13		22		18		2		8		11	
22	19	13	12	22	11	24	12	1	11		12	3	4	15
	11		11		18		10		24		2		4	

1	2	3	4 L	5	6 F	7	8	9	10	11	12 U	13
14	15	16 X	17	18	19	20	21	22	23	24	25	26

MINI SUDOKU

At one time quite a few well-to-do gentlemen employed the services of a butler. In this mini Sudoku, complete the grid so that every row, column and 2x3 box contains the six letters that make up the word 'butler'.

	U			L	
		T			
		B			T
				R	
U	R				
		E			

ANAGRAMS

The following are anagrams of the names of British Prime Ministers. Who are they?

1. He dared what?

2. Me elect talent

3. Brainy lot

4. Random advice

5. Any on the end

WEIRD AND WONDERFUL

Which is the correct definition of these weird and
wonderful words?

1. Wallydrag

a) Headwind
b) Be let down
c) Feeble person

2. Nuncheon

a) Nonchalant
b) A light meal
c) Very small quantity

3. Persiflage

a) Herbal remedy
b) Light-hearted banter
c) Early morning haze

4. Eristic

a) Argumentative person
b) Open-air service
c) Absent-minded

HIDDEN NAMES

A male first name is hidden somewhere in each of the sentences. What is the name?

1. The gentlemen were all generous in giving or donating to the charity.

2. I have full admiration. They all struggle on ardently with little hope of success.

3. The climber noticed the taller alp had a covering of new snow.

4. All he had was salad, hamburger, rye bread with pickle and it was delicious.

5. We were really fortunate when we went to see a performance of *Faust*. In the interval we were taken to meet the cast.

SUDOKU

Fill in all the squares so that each row, column and each
of the 3x3 squares contains all the digits from
one to nine.

		9	2	1			3	
	4				3		5	
		9						6
6		2						
5				3				9
						2		7
4					5			
	9		3				8	
	2			6	1	5		

A PERPLEXING POSER

A chauffeur was heading down a street in Manchester. He went past a stop sign without stopping; he then turned right where there was a 'no right turn' sign and went the wrong way on a one-way street, passing a police car as he went. As he was not breaking any traffic laws, the policemen did not stop him. Why?

WORD LADDER

Well done on having almost completed *The Gentleman's Puzzle Book*. But there is still one puzzle remaining and that is, changing one letter at a time, to turn 'well' into 'done'.

Well

Done

ANSWERS

1. Men of Letters

1 Thomas Hardy, 2 John Keats, 3 William Shakespeare,
4 AA Milne, 5 Roald Dahl.

2. Hidden Names

1 Simon, 2 Neil, 3 Eric, 4 Boris, 5 Eamonn.

3. Weird and Wonderful

1c, 2b, 3a, 4a

4. Word Search: Fish

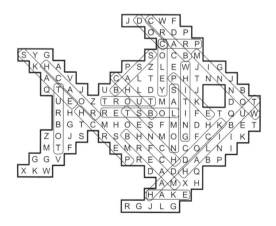

The mystery fish was halibut.

5. Cryptogram
Modern fame is nothing. I'd rather have an acre of land.
Alfred, Lord Tennyson

6. Word Ladder
One possible solution is: good wood word wore wire wine.

7. Word Quest
Acer, acerb, acre, ascribe, basic, brace, briefcase, caber, cafe, care, case, cease, crab, crib, Eric, Erica, fabric, face, facer, farce, fiacre, fierce, race, reface, rice, scab, scar, scare, scarf, scree, scribe.

8. Missing Words
1 note, 2 near, 3 fire, 4 draw, 5 hard.

9. Mini Sudoku

T	I	E	M	Y	L
L	Y	M	E	I	T
E	L	Y	T	M	I
M	T	I	L	E	Y
Y	E	L	I	T	M
I	M	T	Y	L	E

10. Coded Crossword

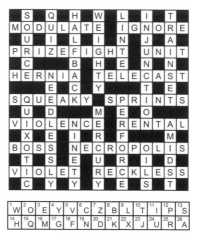

11. Track Word
Post box, bus stop, cafe, newsagent, school, library, litter bin.

12. A Perplexing Poser
A fishing line (or anchor).

13. Sudoku

6	3	7	4	2	9	1	8	5
8	5	4	3	1	6	7	2	9
1	9	2	5	7	8	4	6	3
7	2	8	6	3	1	9	5	4
9	1	6	2	4	5	3	7	8
5	4	3	8	9	7	6	1	2
4	7	5	1	8	3	2	9	6
3	8	9	7	6	2	5	4	1
2	6	1	9	5	4	8	3	7

14. Cryptogram
One of the best things a man can have up his sleeve is
a funny-bone.

15. Anagrams
1 parking meter, 2 traffic lights, 3 speed camera, 4 road works,
5 motorway.

16. Acrostic
1 Podium, 2 Ottawa, 3 Lessen, 4 Impugn, 5 Toffee, 6 Either
The quality of many a gentleman is a 'polite manner'.

17. Matchstick Puzzle

Move the bottom match just a little to create a square
in the centre.

18. Word Quest
Anker, ankh, back, backer, bake, baker, bank, banker, bark, beak,
beck, benchmark, brack, bracken, brake, brank, break, cake,
canker, cark, crake, crank, creak, embank, embark, hack, hacker,
hake, hank, hanker, hark, harken, heck, kerb, kern, khan, knur,
make, maker, mark, nark, neck, rack, rake, rank,
reak, reback, reck.

19. Weird and Wonderful
1b, 2c, 3a, 4a

20. Mystery Sudoku

U	R	H	C	A	L	T	O	S
L	S	T	H	R	O	A	U	C
C	A	O	U	T	S	L	R	H
H	U	C	S	L	A	R	T	O
A	O	S	R	U	T	H	C	L
R	T	L	O	C	H	U	S	A
T	C	A	L	S	U	O	H	R
S	H	U	A	O	R	C	L	T
O	L	R	T	H	C	S	A	U

21. Word Builder
Moustache

22. Ant-ics
1 infant, 2 decant, 3 militant, 4 ignorant, 5 incessant, 6 stagnant

23. Crossword
Across: 6 Custard, 7 Inure, 9 Trio, 10 Ornamental, 11 Football,
13 Runway, 15 Ache, 17 Comma, 18 Grew, 19 Bow tie,
20 Two-piece, 23 Specialist, 26 Item, 27 Darts, 28 Couplet.
Down: 1 Assortment, 2 Pagoda, 3 Eden, 4 Tia Maria, 5 Turn, 6
Cargo, 8 Emanate, 12 Limit, 14 Negligible, 16 Chopped,
17 Crevasse, 21 Output, 22 Crest, 24 Curb,
25 Itch.

24. Word Search: The Gentleman's Puzzle Book

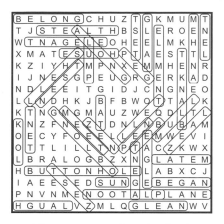

The mystery word was 'anthem'.

25. Coded Crossword

26. Anagrams

1 Paintings, 2 Ornaments, 3 Chandeliers, 4 Medals, 5 Photographs.

27. Mini Sudoku

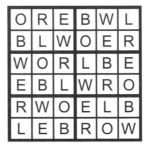

O	R	E	B	W	L
B	L	W	O	E	R
W	O	R	L	B	E
E	B	L	W	R	O
R	W	O	E	L	B
L	E	B	R	O	W

28. Word Ladder

One possible solution is: camp, carp, care, fare, fire.

29. Word Search: European Tour

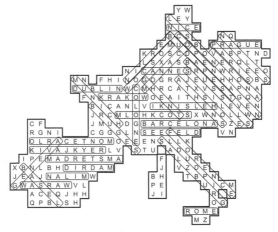

Mystery location: Warsaw

30. Matchstick Puzzle

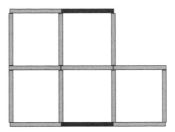

The black matchsticks show the position of the moved matchsticks. One large square has now been created and one smaller one, making a total of six squares.

31. Cryptogram

A gentleman on a train is studying this book. His puzzled look melts into a smile and he turns the page.

32. Mystery Sudoku

R	F	U	M	I	N	H	A	O
H	A	M	O	U	F	I	N	R
N	I	O	A	R	H	F	M	U
O	M	H	N	A	I	R	U	F
A	R	F	U	H	M	O	I	N
U	N	I	F	O	R	M	H	A
F	H	N	R	M	U	A	O	I
I	U	A	H	F	O	N	R	M
M	O	R	I	N	A	U	F	H

33. Weird and Wonderful

1c, 2a, 3b, 4b

34. Hidden Names
1 Anton (or Antony), 2 Alan, 3 Toby, 4 Steve, 5 Damon –
and the name Sid appears as well!

35. Track Word
Pliers, drill, spanner, fork, screwdriver, rake, shears, hammer

36. Word Search: Football Teams

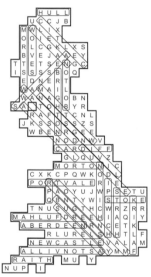

The mystery team is Fulham.

37. Missing Words
1 route, 2 metal, 3 track, 4 house, 5 point.

38. A Perplexing Poser
The sentence should read, 'The notable surgeon was not able to
perform the operation because he had no table.'

39. Criss Cross: Apparel

40. Anagrams
1 Nicholas, 2 Lawrence, 3 Matthew, 4 Christopher, 5 Alastair.

41. Mini Sudoku

O	B	E	I	W	T
T	W	I	B	E	O
B	I	W	T	O	E
E	O	T	W	B	I
I	E	B	O	T	W
W	T	O	E	I	B

42. Word Ladder
One possible solution is: left, loft, loot, look, hook.

43. Ant-ics
1 petulant, 2 remnant, 3 contestant, 4 significant, 5 exorbitant, 6 arrogant.

44. Mystery Sudoku

C	E	M	H	T	A	I	R	L
T	I	H	C	R	L	A	E	M
R	L	A	I	M	E	H	C	T
A	R	E	L	C	T	M	I	H
I	H	L	R	A	M	C	T	E
M	C	T	E	I	H	L	A	R
H	A	I	M	E	R	T	L	C
L	T	R	A	H	C	E	M	I
E	M	C	T	L	I	R	H	A

45. Weird and Wonderful
1c, 2b, 3c, 4a

46. Coded Crossword

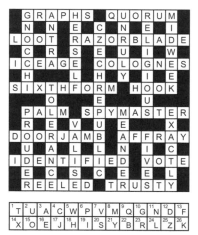

47. Cryptogram

Clothes and manners do not make the man; but when he is made, they greatly improve his appearance.

48. Word Search: Activities and Pastimes

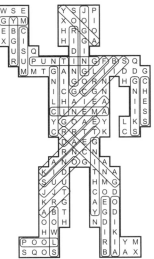

The mystery activity is skiing.

49. Matchstick Puzzle

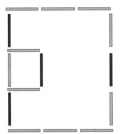

The black matchsticks indicate the position where the matchsticks were moved to in order to create two squares, one inside another.

50. A Perplexing Poser
The letter M.

51. Crossword
Across: 6 Avocado, 7 Excerpt, 9 Adder, 10 Shrinkage, 11 High tea, 13 Spurns, 15 Level crossing, 18 Canopy, 19 Process, 22 Broadcast, 23 Agile, 25 Rosette, 26 Neglect.
Down: 1 Lord, 2 Carrot, 3 Constance, 4 Schnapps, 5 Prearrange, 6 Apathy, 7 Earl, 8 Tress, 12 Greenhouse, 14 Competent, 16 Expedite, 17 Assent, 18 Caber, 20 Orange, 21 Dame, 24 Idea.

52. Word Quest
Chew, crew, phew, screw, shew, shipwreck, shrew, skew, spew, swipe, weir, whicker, whip, whir, whisk, whisker, whisper, wick, wicker, wipe, wiper, wire, wise, wiser, wish, wisher, wisp, wreck, wrick.

53. Sudoku

2	4	3	1	8	6	9	7	5
5	7	1	3	9	2	8	6	4
9	6	8	7	4	5	2	1	3
4	8	5	6	1	3	7	2	9
7	1	9	5	2	4	6	3	8
6	3	2	9	7	8	4	5	1
1	9	6	4	5	7	3	8	2
8	5	7	2	3	9	1	4	6
3	2	4	8	6	1	5	9	7

54. Missing Words
1 sharp, 2 touch, 3 house, 4 piano, 5 scale.

55. Word Builder
Clipboard.

56. Word Search

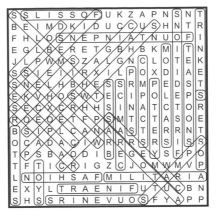

57. Anagrams
Edward Elgar, David Bowie, Sean Connery, Daniel Craig, Paul McCartney.

58. Track Word
Broker, solicitor, pilot, surveyor, doctor, chemist, optician.

59. Word Ladder
One possible solution is: cold, colt, celt, felt, feet, beet, beer.

60. Cryptogram
The finest clothing made is a person's skin, but, of course, society demands something more than this.
Mark Twain

61. Weird and Wonderful
1a, 2b, 3c, 4c

62. A Perplexing Poser
All the people on the boat were married.

63. Word Quest
Aggro, agog, argy, eggy, ergo, gage, gape, gayer, gear, geography, goer, gopher, gore, gorge, gory, grape, grapey, graph, gray, grey, grog, grope, gyre, hypogeal, ogre, orgy, page, phage, porgy, prog, rage, raggy, yoga, yogh.

64. Mystery Sudoku

R	E	D	N	U	X	P	T	O
N	U	P	T	D	O	R	X	E
O	T	X	P	R	E	U	D	N
E	X	T	O	N	U	D	R	P
D	N	O	X	P	R	E	U	T
U	P	R	D	E	T	N	O	X
P	O	N	U	X	D	T	E	R
T	D	E	R	O	P	X	N	U
X	R	U	E	T	N	O	P	D

65. Missing Letters
1 ead – leading, deaden, meadow, 2 rip – scripture, prescript, stripe, 3 ave – bravely, quaver, heaven, 4 low – flower, allowed, glowingly, 5 egi – register, region, strategic.

66. Word Ladder
One possible solution is: meal, teal, tell, till, tile, time.

67. Anagrams
1 black shoes, 2 dinner jacket, 3 cufflinks, 4 aftershave, 5 passport.

68. Coded Crossword

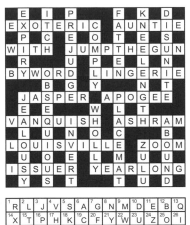

69. Criss Cross: *The Gentleman's Puzzle Book*

70. Matchstick Puzzle

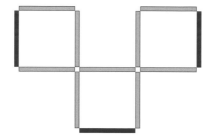

The moved matchsticks are shown in black,
creating three squares.

71. A Perplexing Poser
Peace.

72. Weird and Wonderful
1b, 2c, 3a, 4c

73. Cryptogram
You can tell a lot about a fellow's character by his way
of eating jellybeans.
Ronald Reagan

74. Sudoku

6	8	7	9	3	1	2	4	5
5	3	9	2	7	4	1	8	6
2	4	1	5	8	6	9	3	7
8	2	6	4	9	3	7	5	1
7	5	3	1	2	8	4	6	9
9	1	4	6	5	7	3	2	8
4	6	5	3	1	9	8	7	2
3	9	8	7	6	2	5	1	4
1	7	2	8	4	5	6	9	3

75. Word Search

76. Word Ladder

The following is one possible solution: slow, slot, soot, soon, sown, down.

77. Word Builder

Foresight.

78. Mini Sudoku

T	R	H	P	O	Y
O	P	Y	T	R	H
Y	O	T	R	H	P
P	H	R	Y	T	O
H	T	P	O	Y	R
R	Y	O	H	P	T

79. Men of Letters

1 Arthur Conan Doyle, 2 Charles Dickens, 3 Dylan Thomas,
4 Ian Fleming, 5 TS Eliot.

80. Coded Crossword

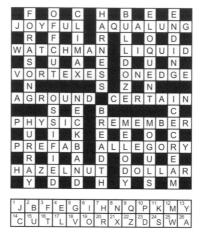

81. Take Away

1. Horatio Nelson, Francis Drake, 2 Steve Redgrave, David
Beckham, 3 Basil Fawlty, Blackadder, 4 George Orwell, Charles
Dickens, 5 Hugh Grant, Colin Firth.

82. Mystery Sudoku

G	K	V	E	N	T	A	L	I
A	E	I	K	G	L	T	V	N
L	T	N	I	V	A	K	E	G
E	L	T	N	K	I	V	G	A
K	N	A	G	L	V	E	I	T
V	I	G	A	T	E	L	N	K
N	V	E	T	A	G	I	K	L
I	A	K	L	E	N	G	T	V
T	G	L	V	I	K	N	A	E

83. A Perplexing Poser
His son.

84. Acrostics
1 Shallow, 2 Cherish, 3 Origami, 4 Tedious, 5 Catwalk,
6 Holiday, with Scotch whisky being what many may appreciate.

85. Cryptogram
Living on Earth is expensive, but it does include a free trip
around the sun every year.

86. Word Search

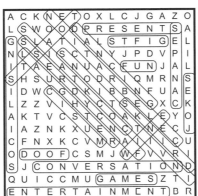

87. Weird and Wonderful
1c, 2b, 3c, 4a

88. Coded Crossword

```
H  P        J     G     D     B
T  O  P  A  Z     B  O  W  L  E  R  H  A  T
   U     N     P     Y     O     Y     N
B  R  I  D  A  L     R  E  V  E  R  S  A  L
   G     E     U     I     E     O     L
G  L  I  M  P  S  E  D     B  I  T  E
   A     I           E     O           T
P  S  Y  C  H  I  C     O  X  I  D  I  S  E
   S           N     M           E     E
      K  I  W  I     A  U  T  O  M  A  T  E
   P     N     Q     S     A     E     S
F  L  A  V  O  U  R  S     C  E  N  S  E  R
   E     O     I     I     T     T     F
T  A  L  K  A  T  I  V  E     D  E  A  L  T
   T     E     Y     E           D     Y
```

1 P	2 E	3 W	4 D	5 F	6 U	7 S	8 G	9 J	10 M	11 N	12 A	13 B
14 X	**15 Z**	**16 O**	**17 K**	**18 C**	**19 Y**	**20 T**	**21 R**	**22 I**	**23 L**	**24 Q**	**25 H**	**26 V**

89. Mini Sudoku

E	S	A	L	M	D
L	M	D	S	E	A
D	A	S	M	L	E
M	E	L	A	D	S
S	D	M	E	A	L
A	L	E	D	S	M

90. Hidden Names
1 Basil, 2 Martin, 3 Hugh, 4 Ryan, 5 Arthur.

91. Criss Cross

92. Cryptogram
One of the biggest thrills in life comes from doing a job well.

93. Missing Letters
1 upe – superior, recuperate, grouped, 2 ouc – voucher, toucan, touch, 3 per – disperse, desperate, repertory, 4 ale – dialect, revealed, talent, 5 ini – clinic, infinity, finish.

94. Word Search: Your Good Health!

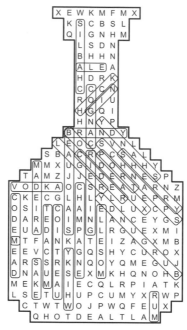

The mystery tipple was whisky.

95. Sudoku

7	2	3	1	8	5	4	9	6
6	9	1	4	3	2	8	5	7
4	8	5	7	9	6	1	2	3
8	5	6	3	7	9	2	1	4
9	3	4	6	2	1	5	7	8
1	7	2	5	4	8	6	3	9
3	6	7	2	1	4	9	8	5
5	1	9	8	6	7	3	4	2
2	4	8	9	5	3	7	6	1

96. A Perplexing Poser

Too wise you are, two wise you be; I see you are too wise for me.

97. Mini Sudoku

A	L	V	E	T	R
R	T	E	A	L	V
T	V	A	R	E	L
L	E	R	V	A	T
E	R	L	T	V	A
V	A	T	L	R	E

98. Mystery Crossword

Across: 1 Beard, 6 Utter, 7 Rhone, 8 Sends, 9 Tress.
Down: 1 Burst, 2 Ether, 3 Atone, 4 Rends, 5 Dress.

99. Coded Crossword

1 B	2 W	3 G	4 Q	5 U	6 E	7 Z	8 F	9 O	10 L	11 T	12 J	13 Y
14 I	15 D	16 M	17 V	18 A	19 R	20 C	21 K	22 H	23 S	24 N	25 P	26 X

100. A Perplexing Poser
You are a postman (or post office).

101. Word Ladder
One possible solution is: rare, fare, fire, fine, find.

102. Hidden Names
1 Russell, 2 Ralph, 3 Edwin, 4 Leslie (and Don!), 5 Walter.

103. Weird and Wonderful
1c, 2b, 3a, 4a

104. Word Quest
Agee, agent, aglet, angel, angle, eagle, eaglet, elegant, entangle, gale, game, gamete, gannet, gate, gateman, gene, genet, gent, gentle, gentleman, glam, gleam, glean, glee, gleeman, legate, legman, legmen, mage, magnet, manege, mange, mangle, mega, melange, ménage, negate, tang, tangle.

105. Missing Letters
1 eac – beacon, deacon, peace, 2 lit – blithely, humility, military, 3 wor – byword, reworking, sword, 4 thi – bathing, soothing, gothic, 5 orr – sorry, torrid, worried.

106. Acrostics
1 Guess, 2 Route, 3 Opera, 4 Units, 5 Salvo, 6 Eaten, with the time of year being the Grouse Season.

107. Mystery Sudoku

T	U	H	L	G	O	E	R	M
M	R	L	U	E	H	G	T	O
O	E	G	M	R	T	H	U	L
L	T	R	H	O	U	M	E	G
G	O	U	R	M	E	T	L	H
H	M	E	G	T	L	R	O	U
U	L	M	E	H	R	O	G	T
R	H	O	T	L	G	U	M	E
E	G	T	O	U	M	L	H	R

108. Jumbled Motors

1 Accelerator, dashboard, 2 seatbelt, ignition, 3 steering wheel,
brake drum, 4 clutch, radiator, 5 headlight, battery.

109. Word Search: Etiquette

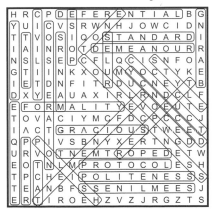

110. Cryptogram

I refuse to join any club that would have me as a member.
Groucho Marx

111. Missing Words

1 master, 2 custom, 3 measure, 4 still, 5 dress.

112. Criss Cross: Names

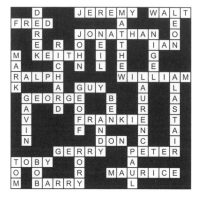

113. Coded Crossword

114. Mini Sudoku

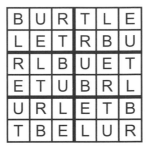

B	U	R	T	L	E
L	E	T	R	B	U
R	L	B	U	E	T
E	T	U	B	R	L
U	R	L	E	T	B
T	B	E	L	U	R

115. Anagrams
1 Edward Heath, 2 Clement Attlee, 3 Tony Blair, 4 David Cameron, 5 Anthony Eden.

116. Weird and Wonderful
1c, 2b, 3b, 4a

117. Hidden Names
1 Gordon, 2 Leonard, 3 Ralph, 4 Gerry, 5 Austin.

118. Sudoku

7	5	9	2	1	6	4	3	8
2	4	6	7	8	3	9	5	1
3	1	8	9	5	4	7	2	6
6	8	2	1	7	9	3	4	5
5	7	4	6	3	2	8	1	9
9	3	1	5	4	8	2	6	7
4	6	3	8	9	5	1	7	2
1	9	5	3	2	7	6	8	4
8	2	7	4	6	1	5	9	3

119. A Perplexing Poser
The chauffer was walking.

120. Word Ladder
One possible solution is: well, dell, doll, dole, done. If you have found another way, well done!

ACKNOWLEDGEMENTS

This book has been a joy to compile and I hope too that it will have brought you some joy (tinged perhaps with a few perplexing moments) as well.

In compiling these puzzles I have been nobly assisted and encouraged by many. My family, Ros, Richard and Emily have, as always, been supportive and game to tackle conundrums and test ideas. Barbara Smith, Mary Pooley and David Finnerty have also kindly given great input. Thanks too to my editor at Summersdale, Chris Turton, and to Caroline Hodgson – both have been most attentive and thorough.

And I also take this opportunity of thanking you for your interest in this book and your support. This I much appreciate.

Neil Somerville

He dent (anag) (3,3)

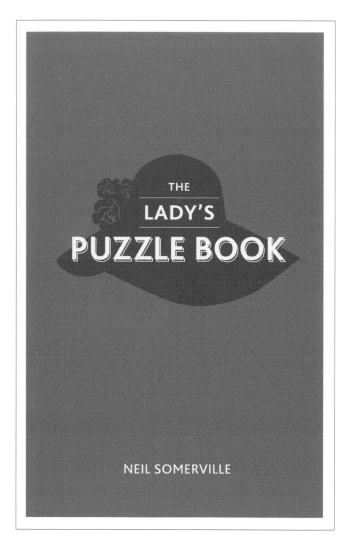

THE
LADY'S
PUZZLE BOOK

NEIL SOMERVILLE

THE LADY'S PUZZLE BOOK

Neil Somerville

£9.99

Hardback

ISBN: 978-1-84953-593-9

For your pleasure and amusement we present *The Lady's Puzzle Book*, a charming little volume filled with enough crafty conundrums to keep any modern lady thoroughly engaged and entertained in everyday moments of idleness or ennui.

THE
BRITISH
PUZZLE BOOK

NEIL SOMERVILLE

THE BRITISH PUZZLE BOOK

Neil Somerville

£9.99

Hardback

ISBN: 978-1-84953-477-2

Test your puzzle skills and brush up on your knowledge of Old Blighty with *The British Puzzle Book*, a charming volume packed with enough crafty conundrums to keep you thoroughly entertained, at home or abroad!

If you're interested in finding out more about our books,
find us on Facebook at **SUMMERSDALE PUBLISHERS** and
follow us on Twitter at **@SUMMERSDALE.**

WWW.SUMMERSDALE.COM